To Ward Botsford,
on whom I lean, and vice-versa

Art direction by Carlo De Lucia

Text copyright © 1984 by Isaac Asimov
Illustrations copyright © 1984 by Wally Neibart

Library of Congress Cataloging in Publication Data

Asimov, Isaac. 1920–
    Isaac Asimov's Limericks for children.
    Summary: A collection of forty-two limericks.
    1. Limericks.   2. Children's poetry, American.
[1. Limericks.   2. American Poetry]   I. Neibart,
Wally, ill.   II. Title.   III. Title: Limericks for
children.
PS3551.S5L55   1984   811'.54   83-23987
ISBN 0-89845-239-2
ISBN 0-89845-240-6 (library)

Published by Caedmon, New York
Printed in the U.S.A.   First Edition

10 9 8 7 6 5 4 3 2 1

ISAAC ASIMOV'S
LIMERICKS
FOR
CHILDREN

Illustrated by Wally Neibart

caedmon

New York

Expensive

A large income becomes fundamental

When you live in a place with high rental.

If your landlord says, "Pay!"

And you ask for delay,

His expression is seldom quite gentle.

Generous

A wealthy young lass named Vanessa

Once said to her father confessa,

"I don't think it's funny

"To give away money."

And all I can say is, "God blessa!"

Apprehension

I get the most curious feeling

Whenever I look at the ceiling.

My Dad says it won't fall

Or annoy me at all,

But why does the plaster keep peeling?

Self-reliance

Young Susan had reached a decision,

Avoiding her teachers' derision.

She proceeded to yelp

To her father, "Don't help!"

And that's how she learned long division.

Affectionate

The mistletoe custom on Christmas

Is something I don't want to miss, Miss.

If I stand on the dot

That marks the right spot,

Will you come here and give me a kiss, Miss?

Hope

I have written a great many books;

I have style, also brains and good looks.

So please acquiesce

(I mean, just say, "Yes!")

To a date, for I'm on tenterhooks!

Racing

A young athlete who lived in Beirut

Ran the mile in his best Sunday suit.

The result, you can guess,

Was a wet, wrinkled mess,

And he ended up second, to boot.

Mistakes

There is one thing, when typing, that vexes

That industrious fellow, Alexis.

There is xxxxx small cause for bliss

When his xxxx work looks like this.

It seems xxx messy with that xxxx many *x*'s.

Weariness

"Come on in," said Theresa, "let's step it.

We will dance and have fun; let us pep it!"

"I can't," said her date,

"It's getting too late,

And I'm feeling a little decrepit."

Uncertainty

Some roses are red, it is true,

And violets often are blue,

And people repeat

That sugar is sweet,

But, dear, I don't know about you.

Gamble

A young risk-taking fellow named Jim

Made a bet—and he's out on a limb.

"Sure, a turtle," he'd say,

"Beats a hare any day."

So his chances of winning are slim.

Directions

If you want to become number one

And make sure everybody has fun,

Just be nice and sweet,

Don't lie and don't cheat,

And don't act like Attila the Hun!

Poverty

These days, at the house where I'm boarding,

There's little I can be affording.

The furniture's old,

The room is ice-cold,

And mealtimes are *quite* unrewarding.

18

Inattention

There was a young woman named Linda

Who loved looking out of the winda.

Her stove, I might mention,

Got little attention,

Burning most of her meals to a cinda.

Pain

I suppose that it's all right to grumble

After stubbing your toe makes you stumble,

But I'm sure that your scream

Will be much more extreme

If you sit on a bee that's a bumble.

Drawback

When it's spring and the sun's shining brightly,

And it turns out that you're feeling spritely,

You will dance, with a smile,

But for just a short while,

If your shoes fit a little too tightly.

Cooking

There once was a bad-tempered boor

Whose orders were always obscure.

His wife never knew

What he'd want in the stew.

It made her feel quite insecure.

21

Justice

It's so strange that you pamper your head

Every time that you get into bed.

While your head does the talking,

It's your feet do the walking,

So put *them* on the pillow instead!

Flowers

It's a sure sign a fellow is lazy,

When he talks about love to a daisy.

"She loves me; she does not"

Daisies *don't* know a whole lot!

If you don't ask the girl, you are crazy!

Heartbreaker

There's a certain young lady named Robyn

Whose notion of life is hob-nobbin'

With some good-looking men,

Pick just one of them, then

Leave all of the rest of them sobbin'.

Punishment

A determined young hunter named Bruce

Took his rifle in search of a moose,

But they weren't in season,

And that tells you the reason

He is now in the town calaboose.

Frustration

There was a young lady named Flo

Who wondered what made her watch go.

She took it apart

And now it won't start,

So I guess that she never will know.

Unreasonable

If you bang on your drum without pause,

It will seem you are breaking no laws.

Yet your parents will shout

And chase you about,

And you'll certainly get no applause.

Kindness

How dearly I love my pet mice!

I make their lives comfy and nice.

They make nests in my shirts

And they eat my desserts.

I don't care—it's called self-sacrifice.

27

Puzzle

That Oliver Twist is a bore;

He always keeps asking for more.

Surely only a fool

Would keep wanting more gruel.

What can he be using it for?

Warning

Do not trust that immense crocodile

As it rests on the banks of the Nile,

And you'd better start running

When he's finished his sunning

And opens his jaws in a smile.

Disaster

A soft-spoken fellow named Lloyd

Once found that his home was destroyed

By lightning and fire

In a horrible pyre.

He said, "I am rather annoyed."

Seasons

They say that the shores of Lake Erie,

In winter look icy and dreary.

In the summer, I've found,

It's the other way 'round,

For everything then seems quite cheery.

Collision

If two skaters should chance to collide,

Interrupting their smooth, steady slide,

And should tumble and fall

And be pushed to the wall,

They can't help but seem undignified.

Ugly

Almost all of the village kids jeered

At a man with green streaks in his beard.

That wasn't quite right,

It was *most* impolite,

But I sure must admit he looked weird.

Loss

There was a young lass named Nanette

Who once made a very large bet

That elephants fly

On the Fourth of July,

And now she is deeply in debt.

Fright

There are few things I fear quite as much as

The proud scorn of an angry old duchess.

I turn blue to my toes

When she turns up her nose.

Won't you help me get out of her clutches?

Dieting

Please do not ask me what is the matter;

There is all this good food on the platter.

Just inhaling the smell

Will be making me swell,

And I'll quickly grow fatter and fatter.

Teen-ager

I must soon have a very large loan

For the bills on my dear telephone,

Or they'll stop all the service,

And the thought makes me nervous.

I can't *live* if there's no dial tone.

Dancing

On a dance floor, a man from Durango

Went and slipped on the peel of a mango.

He fell on his head,

And everyone said,

"What a truly magnificent tango!"

Rescue

An astronaut lost on the moon

Was found not a moment too soon.

There's no water or air

Or anything there,

And it gets pretty hot around noon.

40

Name

Do not ever feel you must show shame

When you're asked to tell people your name.

Though it's hard to pronounce,

You should say it with bounce,

Just as though you're the creme de la creme.

Uncivilized

There was once a young man named O'Neill

Who would kick, bite and scratch with great zeal.

When told to desist

And just use his fist,

He would say boxing wasn't genteel.

41

Old-fashioned

There was an old man of Bangkok

Who had a most curious clock,

The old-fashioned kind

You can no longer find,

With a winder, and hands, and tick-tock.

Nobility

Said the servant, in heated rebuke,

To his master, the surly old duke,

"If your parents were mine,

'Twould be *I* drinking wine.

You are just a genetical fluke."

Vicious

Can a man, do you think, subdivide

Into Jekyll and bad Mr. Hyde?

If that be the case,

Then you're a disgrace—

You've left Jekyll entirely untried.

Equality

One person may well be a rat,

Another an aristocrat.

Be they what they may,

Let each have his say,

For that's where democracy's at!